THE ULTIMATE
AVOCADO
COOKBOOK

THE ULTIMATE
AVOCADO
COOKBOOK

50 MODERN, STYLISH & DELICIOUS RECIPES TO FEED YOUR AVOCADO ADDICTION

COLETTE DIKE

♥

TRANSLATION BY JASMINE VAN DEN HOEK

Skyhorse Publishing

THE MAKING OF

#BREAKFAST

1

#BRUNCH AND LUNCH

2

#DINNER

#LATE-NIGHT SNACKS & DIPS

#SWEETS

This cookbook will give you some insight into my life, which is dominated by cooking, eating, styling, Instagram, and lots of avocados. I was just twelve years old when I created my first little black book filled with recipes. Eating and styling have since remained a passion of mine, resulting in Fooddeco, an Instagram account and daily blog where I share the most delicious recipes.

Fooddeco is a love story between good food and food styling. A way to let people see that food can look beautiful, without having to put in too much effort.

I find inspiration in everything around me, in the smallest details. My friends are happy when I present them with a new dish, and their enthusiastic responses continue to inspire me again and again. I often take well-known recipes and present them with a twist. I use avocados in a lot of recipes such as my breakfast pizza, sushicado, or golden green avocado fries because they are healthy, taste good, and beautiful to look at. You can present this green fruit in a number of ways: from avocado ribbons to avocado roses or avocado polka dots.

Have you fallen in love with avocado like I have? Then be sure to follow @fooddeco and share your creations using this special fruit with me on Instagram using the hashtag #fooddecoavocado.

I am cooking | I am eating | I am shopping | I am styling | I am avo... FOODDECO

ABOUT AVOCADO

This book is for the real avocado fan who is searching for new and original recipes. Most recipes in this book are healthy and vegetarian, and some are vegan. You can make savory or sweet snacks with avocado, like avocado fries or avocado brownies. Aside from being absurdly delicious, avocados are also very photogenic. This bright green fruit allows you to effortlessly make an eye-catching dish.

The avocado is a fruit from an avocado tree, primarily found in South and Central America. The fruits don't start growing until the tree has been planted for five years, but once they grow, they grow in abundance: between 150 and 500 fruits at once. They're available all year round and because of the avocado's uneven skin and pear-like shape it is often referred to as the crocodile pear. Because of its enormous popularity in Mexico, it is referred to as *oro verde*, or green gold.

In the supermarket you will often see people, one after the other, squeezing avocados in the aisle. This is unfortunate, as squeezing bruises the avocados, causing them to turn brown and ripen quickly. You should treat your avocados as carefully as you would an egg.

A good way to tell if an avocado is ripe is to remove the remainder of the stem. If you see a clear green color underneath, this means you've got a winner. If the color is brown or green with spots, the avocado is likely overripe or spoiled. If you can hardly remove the stem, the avocado is definitely not ripe enough. If you want your avocados to ripen quicker, you should leave them in your fruit bowl between the bananas and the apples. Want to keep the avocado you cut in half? Leave the pit in and sprinkle the flesh with some lemon juice or leave the avocado in good company with a peeled onion. This helps the avocado hold its taste and beautiful color. If you want your avocado to ripen less quickly, keep it in the fridge.

A ripe avocado has a creamy texture and a light nutty flavor. Because of this, it is a good replacement for meals made with butter, mayonnaise, cream, or milk or for people who have cow's-milk allergies. Avocados contain a high percentage of unsaturated, good fats (omega 3), which can positively affect your cholesterol levels. They are also packed with vitamin B, iron, potassium, and protein. These great attributes make avocados an affordable superfood.

In this cookbook you will find meals in which avocados play the lead or an important supporting role. In any role, the avocado is the hero of the dish.

Fooddeco ♥ avocado with breakfast, brunch, lunch, and dinner, and even in snacks, desserts, toppings, salads, sushi, pizza, tarts, sauces, and dips.

WHAT YOU'LL NEED

Fooddeco Flavorites

You'll notice that aside from avocado, I use a lot of other ingredients in abundance. As a flavoring, sushi vinegar takes the number one spot. It is a combination of rice vinegar, sugar, and salt. This vinegar is available in any Asian supermarket and in some local supermarkets. Sushi vinegar is usually used to flavor the rice in sushi, but I use it to create dressings and sauces. In addition, there are other flavorings and staple ingredients that often appear in this book, and so, here is an overview. If you have these at home, you'll always be able to make a tasty treat.

IN THE PANTRY:
Olive oil, coconut oil, sushi vinegar, light soy sauce, siracha (spicy chili sauce), yellow curry paste, tahini, mayonnaise, yellow mustard, nuts, dates, cocoa powder, almond flour, panko bread crumbs, quinoa (preferably black or tricolor), sesame seeds (white and black), chili flakes, salt and pepper, tortillas, sesame oil, dried rose petals.

IN YOUR FRIDGE:
Feta cheese, eggs

IN YOUR FREEZER:
Phyllo pastry, frozen fruit

IN YOUR PANTRY:
Avocado, sprouts/watercress (sprout vegetables, can be replaced with alfalfa), bananas, limes, brown sourdough or spelt bread, protein (meat, fish, or chicken)

FOODDECO MUST-HAVES:
It all starts with ingredients and a little bit of creativity, and you'll also need the right kitchen aids.

MY ESSENTIALS:
Sharp knives (Japanese), vegetable slicer, melon baller, straws (preferably wide), frying pan, grill pan with deep grooves (for nice grill marks), blender, food processor, cheese slicer, spatula

♥ Always mash your avocado with a fork to maintain a coarser texture with a bit of a bite. This especially makes savory dishes taste much better. In sweet recipes, be sure to purée your avocado with a blender or in a food processor.

THE MAKING OF. . .

The beautiful color and structure of avocados enable you to make beautiful things. They are perfect for a romantic breakfast, bar snack, or a dinner at home.

Discover how to make an avocado rose, avocado ribbons, mini avocado roses, avocado polka dots, and mini avocado polka dots. For this you will need to use a ripe, but not too soft, firm avocado. Unripe avocados are not flexible enough and also do not taste as good. In addition to this, it is also important to use a sharp knife, a good peeler, and sushi vinegar. The sushi vinegar ensures the avocado stays nice and green, enhances flavor, and gives the avocado a smooth finish.

AVOCADO RIBBONS

ESSENTIAL: (JAPANESE) PEELER

Avocado ribbons came into existence on a summer Sunday afternoon when I wanted to have an avocado sandwich but with a twist. I had never seen it done before but in my household and online it was a huge success.

Remove the skin from the whole avocado, rub it with sushi vinegar, and, using a peeler, cut thin slices from the avocado. They are very frail and vulnerable, so the best way to handle avocado slices is to peel the avocado directly above the dish and carefully pick up the slices.

You will notice that as you get closer to the pit, the slices will become firmer and nicer.

9

1. Choose a ripe avocado.

2. Slice the avocado in half.

4. Coat both halves in sushi vinegar.

5. Cut the avocado into THIN SLICES.

7. Make sure the slices just touch each other.

8. Roll up the slices as shown here.

5. Take out the pit and peel off the skin.

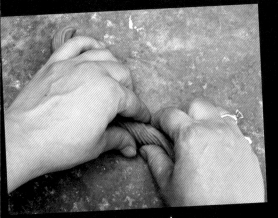

6. Spread out the avocado slices.

7. And . . . FINISHED!

AVOCADO ROSES

ESSENTIAL: SHARP KNIFE

It might seem tedious, but you will be able to create an avocado rose within five minutes. Once you've mastered the art, you will see how easy it is and your roses will keep getting more beautiful.

Cut the avocado in half, remove the pit, and peel the skin. Cover both sides with sushi vinegar and cut the avocado into thin slices. Spread the avocado halves like you see in the photo and roll it back up by moving the avocado rose, carefully, using a spatula.

♥ **You can also make roses with a mango in the same way!**

MINI AVOCADO ROSES

ESSENTIAL: (JAPANESE) PEELER

For this recipe you will need firmer slices of avocado ribbons. Simply roll them up, making sure not to roll it too tight but rather a little looser. This way you will really see the layers of the rose.

AVOCADO POLKA DOTS

ESSENTIAL: MELON BALLER

For this you will need a melon baller; it was developed to make potato balls and is also known by the Dutch and French name *pommes parisienneboortje*. Peel the avocado whole, rub sushi vinegar all over, and scoop out approximately ten balls using the melon baller. Cut these in half, which will leave you with a light green side and a shallow darker side.

♥ **When making avocado polka dots, there are lots of leftovers. The rest of the avocado can be used for an avocado spread or guacamole.**

MINI-AVOCADO POLKA DOTS

ESSENTIAL: STURDY, THICK STRAW

For the miniature polka dots, you will need a straw. This is a remarkable little technique, by the way. First cut the avocado in half, and remove the pit and peel. Insert the straw into the avocado until you hit the cutting board. Remove the straw from the avocado and squeeze the opposite end of the straw until a short bar of avocado falls out. Cut this into as many thin slices as you need. These decorative mini-avocado polka dots are cute on toast, a sandwich, or any appetizers.

1

#BREAKFAST

CROIWAFFLE WITH GUACAMOLE

Serves 1

Waffle iron meets croissant = croiwaffle

1 croissant
Butter
⅔ cup cheese (chedder or Gouda)
Salami (2 or 3 slices)
Fooddeco guacamole (page 65)

ESSENTIAL: WAFFLE IRON

Cut the croissant in half and apply butter to both sides. Grate a substantial amount of cheese on one side and add a few slices of salami. Grate more cheese over the salami and place the other half of the croissant on top.

Place the croissant in the waffle iron on its lowest setting. It is important that it cooks slowly to ensure the outside is crunchy and the cheese is melted within.

In the meantime, make the guacamole (recipe on page 65).

For an extra-cheesy crust, remove the croiwaffle from the waffle iron just before it has finished cooking. Sprinkle some cheese in the waffle iron, place the waffle on top, and sprinkle some additional cheese on top of that. Cook until the outer layer of cheese is golden brown.

♥ **Serve with as much guacamole as you like.**

AVOCADO TOAST

Serves 2

It can't get much simpler than this; toast is
toast. Yet, it still comes down to the right
ingredients and the right equipment. You can
make toast with a toaster, but real avocado
toast is tastiest when cooked in the skillet.

♥ **Avocado toast seems easy but is incidentally
so filling, creamy, and healthy at the same
time. There are so many possible variants
suited for each time of day.**

Use a frying pan or a grill pan. Apply olive oil to
both sides of the bread and grill or fry it (flipping it
every now and again) until the toast is brown with
dark edges. Sourdough bread is best used for this
recipe because of its sponge-like texture and ability
to become crunchy on the outside while staying soft
on the inside. You can also use butter instead of
olive oil.

Tahini spread & avocado ribbons

AVOCADO TOAST WITH TAHINI SPREAD

Tahini is a paste made of sesame seeds from which you can make all sorts of sauces or creams. It is a good replacement for butter or mayonnaise because it's very smooth and full of flavor.

4 small slices brown bread
1 avocado
Sesame seeds to taste

ESSENTIAL FOR THE TAHINI SPREAD
4 tbsp tahini
2 tbsp lemon juice
2 tbsp sushi vinegar
8 tbsp water
2 tsp chili flakes
Optional: 1 clove garlic (finely chopped)

♥ **The garlic is optional because it might still be too early in the day for that!**

Prepare the toast as described on page 16. Meanwhile, make the tahini spread by mixing all tahini spread ingredients in a bowl. Add the tahini spread to the warm toast and place the avocado ribbons (page 8) or mini roses (page 11) on top. Apply the finishing touches by sprinkling sesame seeds on top!

AVOCADO TOAST WITH SOFT-BOILED EGGS AND ANCHOVY CRUMBLE

2 eggs
4 small slices brown bread
1 avocado
Optional: watercress

ESSENTIAL FOR THE ANCHOVY CRUMBLE
1 tin anchovies
2 tbsp olive oil
¾ cup panko bread crumbs

Boil the eggs for approximately six minutes. Prepare the toast as described on page 16. To make the anchovy crumble, melt the anchovy fillets in a skillet with olive oil. Add the bread crumbs to the skillet once the anchovies have melted and cook until the bread crumbs begin to brown. This may take a while.

To assemble the avocado toast, cut the avocado in half and remove the pit and peel. **Smash** the avocado on the toasts, place the peeled and halved soft-boiled eggs on top, and sprinkle the anchovy crumble on top. Add watercress if desired.

AVOCADO TOAST WITH DUKKAH SPICE BLEND

2 slices bread (horizontal slices cut from a round loaf)
2 avocados

ESSENTIAL FOR DUKKAH SPICE BLEND
½ cup Brazil nuts
1 tbsp coriander seeds
2 tbsp cumin
1 tbsp black sesame seeds
1 tbsp fennel seeds
Sea salt and pepper to taste

Mix all of the dukkah ingredients well and toast them in a skillet for approximately ten minutes. Blend all of the ingredients using a blender (not too fine) to a nice mixture. Prepare the toast as described on page 16. Slice one avocado in half, remove the pit, and use a spoon to remove the entire fruit from the peel. Using a fork, mash the avocado finely in a bowl. Spread the avocado mixture on the warm toast and sprinkle a good amount of dukkah over the top. Use the other avocado to make two avocado roses (or something similar).

AVOCADO TOAST WITH CHILI FLAKES AND CHIA SEEDS

4 slices brown bread
1 avocado
Olive oil to taste
Chili flakes to taste
2 tsp chia seeds
Coarse sea salt to taste

Prepare the toast as described on page 16. Meanwhile, slice an avocado in half, remove the pit, and scoop out the flesh of the avocado. Mash this finely in a bowl using a fork. Spread the avocado mixture on warm toast, and sprinkle with olive oil, chili flakes, chia seeds, and coarse sea salt. Within five minutes you will have a delicious, creamy toast with lots of flavor and superfoods!

AVOCADO TOAST WITH FETA SPREAD

4 slices brown bread
¼ cup feta
⅛ cup water
1 avocado
Freshly ground coffee beans
Optional: garlic chives

Prepare the toast as described on page 16. Blend the feta with water with a blender or food processor. If necessary, add more water. Add the avocado and blend to a smooth consistency. Add the whipped avocado and feta spread to the warm toast and sprinkle with freshly ground coffee and *garlic* chives.

♥ A tasty combination with a cup of coffee.

BREAKFAST PIZZA

Serves 2

If you're a pizza lover, you'll be able to eat your favorite food, guilt-free, for breakfast!

1 avocado
2 tsp sushi vinegar
Salt to taste
Coconut or olive oil
2 large tortillas
2 eggs
Lemon juice
Pepper to taste
Optional: garlic chives, chili flakes, and sriracha

Cut the avocado in half, remove the pit, scoop out the flesh, and mash to a smooth consistency in a bowl with sushi vinegar, salt, and some chili flakes.

Grease a frying pan lightly with coconut or olive oil, heat the pan, and bake the tortillas until both sides turn light brown. Set aside. Use the same pan to fry the eggs. Spread the avocado mixture on the warm tortillas and place the fried eggs on top. Add lemon juice, pepper, salt, and garlic chives or sriracha as per your palate.

♥ *Garlic chives* **are a type of watercress. They have a light garlic aroma and can be identified by small black dots on the ends of the cress leaves.**

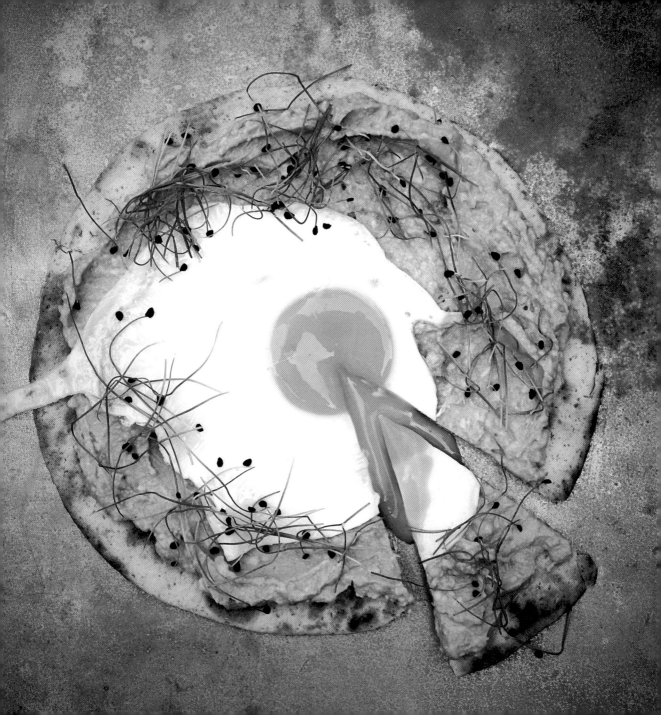

GRANOLA

1 pot

I first made a single serving of granola per week but started making more when my eldest daughter became a big fan. Every morning she now likes to eat her "nola." This recipe variation made with avocado has an extra nutty taste and is delicious when combined with cinnamon.

1 cup rolled oats
1 cup nuts, unroasted
½ cup quinoa, uncooked
1½ cup pumpkin and sunflower seeds

REQUIRED FOR THE SAUCE
⅔ cup honey
3 tbsp coconut oil
2 tbsp sunflower oil
2 large tbsp cinnamon or more to taste
2 avocados, peeled, pitted, mashed

♥ For a vegan version, use maple syrup instead of honey.

Preheat the oven to 350°F. In a saucepan, add honey, coconut oil, sunflower oil, and cinnamon until everything is combined. Add in the mashed avocado and stir until you have a nice smooth sauce. Beware: the sauce will be very hot.

Mix all dry ingredients in a large bowl and add the avocado cinnamon sauce. Make sure that all rolled oats, nuts, quinoa, and seeds are covered with a layer of sauce. Put a piece of baking paper on a large baking sheet and divide the mixture across the sheet. Note: make sure the layer is thin, otherwise your granola will not be crispy.

Put the baking sheet in the oven and bake the granola for 30 minutes until golden brown and crispy. Scoop the mixture every 10 minutes and pay attention during baking because every oven works differently! Remove the granola from the oven and press it with the back of a spoon across your baking sheet: this gives you nice big chunks. Let the granola then completely cool for about 1 hour until it becomes nice and crispy. Break the granola in good-sized chunks and store them in an airtight container.

AVOCADO & COCONUT YOGURT

Serves 2

1 banana (frozen)
1 avocado
½ lime (juice and zest)
1 cup coconut yogurt
Toppings: your favorite yogurt toppings
Toppings as depicted: granola, grated coconut, edible
flowers, dried rose petals, fresh fruit

The night before creating this dish, place a banana in the freezer. The next day, use a sharp knife to cut the peel from the frozen banana and proceed to cut the banana into slices. Cut the avocado in half, and remove pit and peel. Blend banana, avocado, lime juice and zest, and yogurt to a lovely mixture. Top with granola (page 23) and present your dish with multiple toppings of your choosing. Serve nice and cold.

PANCAKE STACK

8 small pancakes

½ cup oats, ground extra fine
1 banana
1 avocado
1 tbsp honey
2 eggs
½ lime (juice and zest), add more to your taste
Salt
Olive or coconut oil, to fry
Toppings: maple syrup or fresh fruit and honey

Blend the oats to a fine consistency. Peel the banana and break it into pieces. Cut the avocado in half, and remove pit and peel. Blend oats and banana with honey, eggs, lime juice and zest, and salt. Grease a frying pan with olive or coconut oil and scoop the batter in small circles into the pan. Cook three to four pancakes at a time, and continue until you have used all the batter. Cook the pancakes slowly and turn over once the bottom of each pancake has turned brown.

♥ **Serve with fresh fruit and honey or maple syrup.**

AVOCADO TOAST WITH TRUFFLE MAYONNAISE

Serves 2

2 slices bread
1 avocado
2 tbsp truffle mayonnaise

Prepare the toast as described on page 16. Meanwhile, halve the avocado and remove the pit and the peel. Slice both halves into thin slices but ensure that the slices are still touching. Spread a heaping tablespoon of truffle mayonnaise on the warm toast.

Place both halves of the avocado with their insides facing the cutting board and press the stop softly so that the avocado slices fan out. Repeat with the other half and using a broad spatula place the avocado on the toast.

♥ A ripe avocado, perfect toast, and truffle mayonnaise: you won't need much more to put a delicious meal on the table.

2

#BRUNCH & LUNCH

TO GO: HEALTHY MASON JAR SALAD

Serves 2

A *healthy jar* salad is an easy and cheap way to create a portable and tasty meal. The order of ingredients is important in this recipe. If you put the dressing on top, you'll end up with a soggy salad. If you finish with the beets, everything will become pink. But, when you build the salad in the right order, it stays perfect. Varieties of this recipe include using different vegetables, types of lettuce, and dressings.

¾ cup black quinoa
1–2 tbsp olive oil
1 tsp cumin
½ tsp chili flakes
Salt and pepper to taste
1 cup cooked beets, finely grated
2 stems fresh mint, including leaves
⅓ cup beet greens
1 avocado
¼ cup pistachios

ESSENTIAL FOR THE FETA DRESSING:
½ cup feta
1 tbsp olive oil
⅓ cup water

ESSENTIAL:
2 glass jars with screw lids, 12 oz.

Cook the quinoa to package instructions. Add olive oil, cumin, chili flakes, salt, and pepper to season.

Meanwhile, in a food processor or blender add all feta dressing ingredients until a silky consistency is reached. Add more water if necessary, and scrape the feta from the sides to the bottom of the bowl and continue this process until the dressing becomes very creamy. Cut the avocado in half, and remove the pit and peel. Slice both halves into thin slices.

Layer the jar in the following order starting from the bottom: Quinoa, beets, feta dressing, mint, avocado, beet greens, nuts.

❤ **Do not fill your jar to the brim, as you will need to shake the salad before you eat it.**

WHIPPED FETA SANDWICH WITH AVOCADO AND MINI ROSES

Serves 2

½ cup feta
¼ cup water
4 slices brown bread
Olive oil to taste
1 avocado

Blend feta and water together using a blender or food processor. If necessary add more water. Scrape the feta from the sides of the bowl to the center until a creamy consistency is formed. Optionally, you can add some lemon juice.

Toast the bread in a frying pan with a bit of olive oil until it is crunchy. Spread the whipped feta on the toast and place the avocado ribbons (page 8) and the mini avocado roses (page 11) on top. Place the roses between the avocado ribbons.

PITA BREAD

6 large or 8 small pita breads

1 cup warm water
1 tbsp dried yeast
1¾ cups flour + extra for kneading
2 tbsp olive oil + extra to taste
2 tsp salt

SERVING SUGGESTIONS (AS SHOWN)
Your favorite guacamole (pages 64–67)
Avocado roses (page 11)
Garlic chives
Broccoli sprouts

Mix the warm water and the yeast in a bowl; let the mixture stand for 5 minutes. In a separate bowl mix the flour with the olive oil and stir until combined. Then, add in the water-yeast mixture, stir well, and knead everything into a smooth dough. Finally, add in the salt and knead for a while. Mix in as much extra flour as needed to ensure that the dough is not sticky. Coat a clean bowl and the ball of dough with olive oil, and lay the ball of dough in the bowl. Cover the bowl with a cloth and let the dough sit for at least 1 hour in a warm place until it has doubled in size. Set your oven on high and shape the dough into 8 balls. Line a baking sheet with baking paper. Place the balls of dough onto the covered baking sheet and press them flat to the size of a pita bread. Bake the breads for 5 to 10 minutes in the oven until they are tender and start to color.

♥ Serve with toast, fresh bread, or salad.

AVOCADO EGG SALAD IN AVOCADO BOWLS

Serves 2

This healthy version of egg salad is tasty and easy. Although the mayonnaise is missing, this egg salad recipe is just as filling and creamy.

3 hard-boiled eggs
2 avocados, 1 for the egg salad and 1 for the bowl
½ lime, juice
Chili flakes to taste
Pepper and salt to taste
Toppings: rose petals, cress, smoked paprika, chopped chives, extra chili flakes

Peel the eggs and cut them in half; keep the egg whites and egg yolks separated. Cut 1 avocado in half and remove the pit. Scoop the flesh out and mix it together with the egg yolks in a bowl. Add the lime juice and chilli flakes, pepper, and salt to taste.

Cut the egg whites into pieces, add them to the egg salad mixture, and stir well. Cut the second avocado in half and remove the pit and the skin. Cut a small piece off the bottom of the avocado halves so that they stay in place. Fill the avocado bowls with the egg salad and sprinkle everything with one or more toppings to your liking.

AVOCADO GARDEN

Serves 2

REQUIRED FOR THE HUMMUS
1 lemon, juice
1 clove garlic, grated
3 tbsp tahini
3 tbsp olive oil
1 (15 oz.) can chickpeas, drained
¼ cup ice cold water

REQUIRED FOR THE AVOCADO GARDEN
1 avocado
Crackers or pita bread (page 33) to serve
Toppings: cumin powder, paprika powder, cress, sesame seeds, chili flakes, broccoli, edible flowers, dried rose petals, lime zest, and juice

Mix the lemon juice in a food processor or blender together with the garlic and blend for 30 seconds. Then, add the tahini and olive oil. Mix everything until you have an even paste-like mixture. Now, add the chickpeas and slowly add in the water. Let the food processor run for a few minutes. Season with salt and possibly some extra lemon juice.

Cut the avocado in half and remove the pit and the peel. Cut a small piece off the bottom of the avocado halves so that they stay in place. Fill the avocado bowls with the hummus and sprinkle with one or more toppings of your choice.

♥ Serve with crunchy crackers or pita bread (page 33).

WATERMELON PIZZA
6 pizzas

A sweet, savory, summery, fresh dish.

1 mini watermelon
1 cup feta
½ cup water
1 avocado
Fresh mint for topping
Pistachios for topping

Slice the mini watermelon in ½-inch pieces. You should end up with approximately six slices. Grill the watermelon on one side without oil. Once grill marks start to appear, remove the watermelon and set aside. Repeat with each slice of watermelon.

Meanwhile, in a food processor or hand blender mix the feta and water together. If necessary, add more water. Scrape the feta from the sides to the center of the bowl and repeat this until you end up with a very creamy mixture. Make the avocado polka dots (page 12), wash the mint, and grind the pistachios coarsely in a mortar and pestle. Spread the whipped feta on the watermelon pizza slices and top with the avocado dots, fresh mint, and pistachios.

RICE CAKES WITH CURRIED HUMMUS & AVOCADO

2 rice cakes

Make this recipe in no time and get a deliciously smooth hummus.

REQUIRED FOR THE HUMMUS
1 lemon, juice
1 clove garlic, grated
3 tbsp tahini
3 tbsp olive oil
1 (15 oz.) can chickpeas, drained
¼ cup ice cold water
1 large tbsp curry powder, roasted in a dry pan
1 tsp turmeric
2 rice cakes
1 avocado
Toppings: black sesame seeds, cress, dried rose petals, lime zest, paprika powder, sea salt, peas

Mix the lemon juice in a food processor or blender together with the garlic and blend for 30 seconds. Then, add the tahini and olive oil. Mix everything until you have an even paste-like mixture. Now, add the chickpeas and slowly add in the water. Then, add in the curry powder and turmeric. Let the food processor run for a few minutes. Season with salt and possibly some extra lemon juice.

Spread the curried hummus on the rice cakes and carefully place your avocado rose (page 11) on top. Decorate your rice cakes with one or more toppings of your choice.

♥ **Possibly the tastiest hummus you have ever made.**

TORTILLA PIZZA WITH SWEET POTATO & AVOCADO RIBBONS

1 pizza

I always have baked sweet potato in my household (the perfect snack for babies)!

1 large whole-grain tortilla
1 sweet potato, oven-baked (make ½-inch notch lengthwise and cook in the oven for 45 minutes at 400°F)
1 tsp cumin
1 tsp paprika powder
Salt and pepper to taste
1 egg
1 avocado
Microgreens for topping

Grill the tortilla in the oven or on a grill plate for a short while. Scoop out the roasted sweet potato from its peel. Mash the sweet potato and mix with cumin and paprika powder. Season with salt and pepper. Meanwhile, heat a frying pan with olive oil and cook an egg. Spread the sweet potato on the wrap and place the fried egg on top. Place avocado ribbons (page 8) on top and decorate your pizza with microgreens.

3

"HIM, RED WINE, CANDLELIGHT, AND AVOCADO"

#DINNER

♥ This soup tastes delicious paired with freshly baked sourdough bread.

GREEN GAZPACHO
Serves 4

1 avocado
½ cucumber, peeled
2 cups vegetable stock, cooled
½ cup olive oil
½ tsp cumin
1 celery rib (including leaves), finely chopped
½ lime, juice
1 clove garlic, finely chopped
Fresh mint leaves (+ some extra for decoration)
1 tbsp sushi vinegar
Salt and pepper to taste
Optional: handful fresh spinach; it will make your soup extra green!

ESSENTIAL FOR DECORATION
Olive oil
Rose petals
Mint leaves
Crushed pistachios
Corn kernels

Place all ingredients except garnishes in a blender and mix to a silky soup texture. Season with salt and pepper. Add more water if the soup is too thick.

Place the gazpacho in the refrigerator for a few hours. Gazpacho is supposed to be served cold. Pour the gazpacho into four bowls and top with a dash of olive oil, rose petals, mint leaves, crushed pistachios, and corn kernels.

SWEET POTATO CHEDDAR SOUP

Serves 2

2 tbsp olive oil
1 white onion, shredded
1 carrot, finely chopped
1 clove garlic, finely chopped
2 tsp cumin
½ tsp cinnamon
1 tsp chili flakes
2–3 (2½ cups) medium sweet potatoes
3 cups chicken stock
1 avocado
1 cup shredded cheddar cheese
Salt and pepper to taste

Heat the olive oil in a pan, add the onion, and cook for about five minutes. Add carrot, garlic, cumin, cinnamon, and chili flakes and fry for two more minutes. Meanwhile peel the sweet potato and cut into pieces. Add the sweet potato and chicken stock to the pan and bring to a boil. Cook for approximately 20 minutes and place all ingredients in a blender and mix to a silky soup texture.

Cut the avocado into two roses (page 11). Add the cheddar to the soup and let it melt. Stir the soup and season with salt and pepper. Pour the soup in a bowl and lay the avocado rose on top.

♥ Serve the silky soup in a shallow bowl, otherwise your rose might sink!

AVOCADO PHYLLO PIZZA WITH SMOKED SALMON

Serves 4 as an appetizer

Phyllo pastry is a great alternative to puff pastry and can effectively be used as a pizza base. Light and crunchy.

8 large sheets phyllo pastry
Olive oil
1 tbsp yellow curry paste
2 tbsp water
4 tbsp mayonnaise
1 avocado
4 oz. smoked salmon
Garlic chives or another type of cress for topping
Poppy seeds or black sesame seeds for topping

ESSENTIAL EXTRAS
Baking paper

Heat the oven to 400°F. Defrost the phyllo pastry and rub four sheets with olive oil. On each sheet, place another sheet of phyllo pastry. Use the lid of a pan to trace a circle from each set of layered pastry sheets. Cut the edges.

Make the pizza base as large as possible so only the corners need to be removed. Bake the pizza bases for 8 to 10 minutes until they are golden brown and crunchy. While the pizzas bake, place something heavy on top of them like another baking tray so that they remain nice and flat. Ensure there is baking paper between the phyllo pastry and the weight so that the pastry does not stick to it. Remove the weight for the last two minutes of baking so that your pizzas can brown on top. Heat the yellow curry paste in a frying pan, add two tablespoons of water to it, and stir into the mayonnaise. Meanwhile, make the avocado polka dots (page 12). Spread the curry mayonnaise on the pizza bases and top with smoked salmon, avocado polka dots, garlic chives, poppy seeds, and sesame seeds. Serve immediately.

VARIATION WITH WHIPPED FETA AND CARPACCIO

For an alternative option, replace the curry mayonnaise with whipped feta (page 32) or replace the salmon with carpaccio.

GOAT CHEESE TRUFFLE

Serves 4

This goat cheese truffle is fun to add to a salad.

NEEDED FOR THE DRESSING
2 tbsp sesame oil
2 tbsp sushi vinegar
2 tbsp light soy sauce
½ shallot, peeled
Salt and pepper to taste

NEEDED FOR THE GOAT CHEESE TRUFFLE
2 avocados
½ cup nuts (pistachios and almonds)
1 tsp chili flakes
½ lime, zest
Sushi vinegar
½ cup soft goat cheese
1 cup lettuce
Optional: bread with olive oil

Mix all ingredients for the dressing with a hand mixer to an even mass. Add salt and pepper to taste and set aside.

Halve the avocados lengthwise and remove the pit and peel. In a food processor grind the nuts, chili flakes, and lime zest to a fine crumble.

Rub the avocados with sushi vinegar. Fill both halves with the goat cheese. Stack the halves on top of each other again. For stability, cut a small piece off the bottom of the avocado.

Roll the whole avocado through the nut mixture and press it lightly with your hand. Set the avocado truffle erect on the plate and sprinkle some of the nut mixture around it. Place the lettuce around the truffle and serve with a side of dressing.

♥ **Instead of goat cheese, you can also use feta. It you're looking for a vegan alternative, try filling the avocados with hummus.**

QUINOA FLOWERPOT
Serves 2

You can use a real flowerpot for this, but a tapas plate is a prettier option. This has the same color and you'll also see a bit more of the "soil" this way.

⅔ cup black quinoa
1 tbsp olive oil
1 tsp cumin powder
1 tsp chili flakes
Salt and pepper to taste
½ cup feta
¼ cup water
1 avocado (for two roses)
Cress
Rosebuds for topping
Rose petals for topping

ESSENTIAL FOR THE ANCHOVY CRUMBLE
1 tin anchovy fillets
2 tbsp olive oil
1 cup panko bread crumbs

EXTRAS
Two flowerpots or two tapas plates

Cook the quinoa according to package instructions, and add extra flavor by mixing with the olive oil, cumin, chili flakes, salt, and pepper.

To make the anchovy crumble, melt the anchovy fillets in two tablespoons of olive oil. Once the anchovies are melted, add the bread crumbs and cook until they begin to color. This can take a while. Make whipped feta by blending the feta with the water in a food processor or by hand. If necessary, add more water and scrape the feta from the sides of the machine to the bottom. Continue to do this until it is very creamy. Scoop a layer of whipped feta into the flowerpots and then divide the quinoa across the two pots. Using the avocado, make two roses (page 11) and lay them on top of the "soil" in your pot. Finish by sprinkling some anchovy crumble, cress, rosebuds, and rose petals on top.

♥ Nice with salmon sashimi or
sushi. For some added variety,
add sesame oil to the dressing.

PICKLED AVOCADO

Serves 4, as a side dish
½ avocado per person

A favorite side dish and a delicious addition with an Asian starter, where the avocado also serves as a bowl for the soy sauce. Very simple, quickly finished, and full of flavor.

3 tbsp finely chopped fresh cilantro with stems
1 lime, zest and juice
2 avocados
Soy sauce to taste
Black sesame seeds to taste

Mix the cilantro, and lime zest and juice in a bowl. Set aside.

Cut the avocados in half and remove the pits and the peels. Cut a small piece off the bottom of the avocado halves so that they stay in place, and add the avocado halves to the bowl with the lime mixture. Rub the lime mixture into the avocado halves well and let them sit in the mixture for about 20 minutes before serving. Lay the avocado bowls pit-half up and pour some soy sauce into the cavity of each pit. Top all with black sesame seeds.

♥ You can use leftover cooked white rice instead of sushi rice.

♥ Vegan? Add mango instead of fish.

SUSHICADO

Serves 4 as an appetizer

½ cup sushi rice
Sushi vinegar to taste
4 avocados (the largest you can get)
4 oz. fresh salmon (sashimi quality), cut in 4 portions
2 baby cucumbers, ends cut off, halved lengthwise
Wasabi to taste
1 nori sheet, cut into 4 pieces
Black sesame seeds to taste
Soy sauce to taste

Cook the sushi rice according to package instructions and season with sushi vinegar. Cut one of the avocados in half lengthwise and remove the pit. With a spoon remove a little extra pulp out of the avocado so that you have as much space as possible for the filling.

Fill the cavity of the avocado with sushi rice, salmon, and cucumber. Coat the sides with wasabi and stick the avocado halves together again. Peel the avocado now and coat with sushi vinegar.

Dampen a nori sheet with water and wrap it around the avocado. Cut a small piece from the bottom of the avocado so that your sushicado sticks together. Finally, roll the avocado in black sesame seeds. Prepare the other 3 avocados the same way and serve them immediately. Serve with soy sauce and extra wasabi.

VEGGIE NOODLES

Serves 4 as a side dish

This dish is small, super fresh, and very simple! This is a great dish to accompany sushi.

½ daikon
1 tbsp sushi vinegar
Black sesame seeds
1 lime, zest
1 avocado

FOR THE DUKKAH SPICE BLEND
½ cup nuts (Brazil nuts)
1 tbsp coriander seeds
2 tbsp cumin
1 tbsp black sesame seeds
1 tbsp fennel seeds
Sea salt and pepper to taste

Combine all the dukkah ingredients and toast them for approximately 10 minutes in the frying pan. The scent will be amazing! Mix all of the ingredients using a blender until it becomes a nice mixture, but make sure it is not too fine.

Peel the daikon and cut it into thin long strips using a vegetable slicer. Combine the daikon, sushi vinegar, black sesame seeds, and lime zest.

Divide the daikon noodles across four small plates and add some avocado ribbons (page 8). You add the avocado near the end of preparation as it is fragile. Sprinkle some dukkah spice and black sesame seed over the top.

CURRIED SALMON BURGER

Serves 2

ESSENTIAL FOR THE BURGER
10 oz. salmon
1 onion, shredded
1 garlic clove, finely chopped
1 tbsp yellow curry paste
3 tbsp bread crumbs
Olive oil for frying

ESSENTIAL FOR THE TOPPINGS
4 slices cheddar cheese
4 hamburger rolls with sesame seeds
1 avocado
Lettuce
Fried onions
Fresh cilantro

ESSENTIAL FOR THE CURRY MAYONNAISE
1 tbsp yellow curry paste
2 tbsp boiled water
3–4 tbsp mayonnaise

Mix the burger ingredients except olive oil using a blender or food processor. Don't blend it too fine; it should be more to the texture of minced meat. Create four burger patties from the salmon mixture, wrap them in cling wrap, and let them set in the refrigerator.

Heat the olive oil in the frying pan. Fry the salmon burgers on each side for 10 minutes until cooked. In the last five minutes, place a slice of cheddar cheese on top. Meanwhile, toast the burger buns in the frying pan or the toaster. Cut the avocado in half, remove the pit and peel, and cut the avocado into slices.

Make the curry mayonnaise by mixing the curry paste with boiled water and adding the mayonnaise to the mixture. Spread the curry mayonnaise on the buns and place each burger on the bottom half of the buns. Top with avocado slices. Finish the salmon burgers off with a leaf of lettuce, an extra dab of mayonnaise, some crunchy fried onions, and cilantro.

♥ Wetting your hands when making the burger patties makes them easier to handle.

AVOCADO BUN WITH BEET BURGER

Serves 4

This avocado burger bun is one of my tastiest and most popular creations. It is now served all over the world! It is still fun to see this recipe circulating on Instagram and even on restaurant menus.

REQUIRED FOR BEET BURGERS (12 SMALL BURGERS)
½ cup quinoa
1 cup raw beets, grated
1¼ cup black beans, drained
1 onion, finely chopped
1 clove garlic, grated
1 red pepper, finely chopped
⅓ cup mushrooms, cleaned and finely chopped
1 tbsp sweet soy sauce
1 tsp Worcestershire sauce
1 tsp nutmeg
1 tsp mustard
Salt and pepper to taste
¼ cup oat flour
Cheddar cheese slices, optional
4 avocados
Sushi vinegar
Your favorite burger sauce, or simply mayonnaise
    and ketchup
1 onion, sliced
1 tomato, sliced
1 thick pickle, sliced
Handful lettuce
White sesame seeds
4 skewers, optional

Boil the quinoa according to package instructions. Grind the beets fine in a food processor. Transfer the beets into a mixing bowl. Then, mix the other beet burger ingredients (except the oat flour) in the food processor until combined. Add in the finely ground beets, then the oat flour, and stir everything well. Refrigerate for 30 minutes, then form 12 sturdy burger patties.

Preheat the oven to 430°F. Cover one baking sheet with baking paper and coat with oil. Place the 12 beet patties on top and bake the burgers about 15 minutes per side in the oven. If adding cheese, place on top of the burgers in the last 5 minutes of baking. Meanwhile cut the avocados in half lengthwise and remove the pits and the shells. Coat the avocado halves with sushi vinegar. Cut a small piece off the bottom of the avocado halves so that the avocado buns stay in place.

Start building your burger. Add your condiment(s) of choice in the two cavities of the avocado. On the lower half of the avocado bun with beet burger, add sliced onion, tomato, pickle, and some lettuce. Then, add the top of the avocado bun on top and sprinkle with sesame seeds to achieve the avocado-burger-bun effect! Repeat with the other 3 avocados.

♥ If your burger does not stand well, vertically poke a skewer through the entire burger to hold it together.

♥ No time to make your own burger patties? Sub in your favorite store-bought veggie, beef, or salmon patty.

♥ Serve the burgers with tortilla chips for a nice bite.

STUFFED TOMATO

Serves 4 as an appetizer

4 tomatoes, good quality
Balsamic glaze to taste
Olive oil
4 basil leaves as the "stems" for the tomatoes
Salt and pepper to taste

ESSENTIAL FOR THE FILLING
1 slice (old) white bread
1 tbsp olive oil + extra to taste
½ tsp garlic powder
Salt and pepper to taste
2 tbsp capers
1 tbsp olives
1 tin anchovies, finely cut

ESSENTIAL FOR THE AVONNAISE
1 avocado, peeled and pitted
4 tbsp olive oil
2 tbsp sushi vinegar
2 tsp mustard
1 can tuna, finely sliced

Place a large pot of water with a dash of salt on the stove and bring to a boil. Wash the tomatoes and remove the stems and crowns. Slice a small shallow cross on the bottom of each tomato. Blanch the tomatoes in the boiling water for approximately one minute, depending on the size of each tomato, until the skin starts to tear (the tomatoes should absolutely not cook through), then place them in cold water. Peel them and put them aside, covered, in the refrigerator for at least one hour.

For the filling, slice the bread into small squares and fry it in in the frying pan with the olive oil, garlic powder, salt, and pepper until golden brown and crispy. Put aside.

To make the avonnaise, in a bowl mix the avocado with olive oil, sushi vinegar, and mustard to a completely smooth, mayonnaise-like substance. Season with salt and pepper. Slice the tuna as fine as possible.

Remove the tomatoes from the refrigerator. Cut a slice off the top of each tomato. Remove the core and scoop the fruit out using a small spoon. Hollow out the tomatoes as much as possible.

Divide the tuna across four plates in the middle of each dish. Scoop a thick layer of avonnaise to cover all the tuna. Toss the filling with the capers, olives, anchovies, and some olive oil. Scoop this blend into the hollow tomatoes. Place the tomato on top of the layer of avonnaise. Brush the tomatoes with olive oil and place a small basil leaf on top to re-create the tomato's stem. Decorate this dish with balsamic glaze in a nice pattern and serve immediately.

♥ This image does not depict the balsamic glaze.

RAW BROCCOLI SALAD

Serves 4 as a large appetizer

Broccoli stems are perfect to eat cooked, steamed, baked, or in this case raw, in a salad. Delicious!

2 cups broccoli heads and stems
3 tbsp truffle oil (+ extra)
Salt to taste
4 eggs
⅛ cup almond shavings
2 avocados
¾ cup young, soft goat cheese
Optional: fresh truffle shavings or truffle tapenade

Wash the broccoli and break or slice the tops from the stems. Steam or cook the tops al dente, and julienne the stems (raw). Drain the broccoli tops, rinse them with cold water, and let them dry (optionally you can squeeze out some of the extra liquid). Add the raw stem slices and season with truffle oil and salt.

Meanwhile, boil the eggs for six minutes, depending on the size, until they are soft boiled. Roast the almond shavings in a dry frying pan until golden brown. Halve the avocados and remove the pits and peels. Cut into four avocado roses (page 11).

Divide the broccoli across four plates. Add the avocado roses, boiled eggs, almond shavings, and goat cheese. Sprinkle with additional truffle oil and salt. For added decadence add truffle shavings or fresh truffle tapenade.

FRESH AVOCADO TARTARE AND COQUILLE

Serves 8

8 scallops
8 slices ham (long slices, optionally some serrano ham
   as depicted)
3 avocados
3 Granny Smith apples
½ lemon, juice
1 tbsp olive oil
Salt and pepper to taste
Balsamic glaze or balsamic vinegar pearls
Butter, for frying

Take the fresh scallops and ham out of the refrigerator
and let sit for 15 minutes. Peel and pit the avocados
and apples. Cut the avocados and apples in small,
even cubes.

Season with lemon juice, olive oil, salt, and pepper.
Toss the ingredients gently. Divide the ingredients
across eight plates and apply a bit of pressure to the
tartare to make the mixture sturdier. Wrap the long
slices of ham around the tartare.

Dab the scallops dry and cook them evenly on both
sides in a little bit of butter until golden brown. Place
the scallop on top of the tartare and sprinkle some
balsamic glaze around it. Balsamic vinegar pearls are
even prettier.

♥ For a nice crust, massage the
scallops with salt. Let the salt
absorb somewhat before cooking.

4

#LATE-NIGHT
SNACKS & DIPS

GUACAMOLE

Nothing can really go wrong when you make guacamole. Mash the avocado with your favorite herbs and spices. Varying the ingredients enables you to discover alternatives on top of the base recipe.

Mash your homemade guacamole with a fork for the best texture and taste.

♥ I prefer to use a whole lime, but if this is too intense for you, half a lime will be plenty.

FOODDECO GUACAMOLE

There are endless varieties to guacamole, and everybody usually has their own favorite base recipe. This is mine: spicy with lots of herbs and a nice touch of acidity.

2 avocados
1 lime, juice and zest
1 tsp chili flakes
Handful cilantro, finely chopped (4 tbsp)
1 spring onion, shredded
1 garlic clove, shredded
Sea salt to taste
Toppings of your choice: Pickled ginger, edible flowers, cress, pomegranate seeds, and tortilla chips to serve

Halve the avocados and remove the pits and peels. Place the avocados in a bowl and mash them using a fork. Add in all other ingredients. Make it as coarse or as smooth as you like. Taste and add more salt or chili flakes if necessary.

Pairs well with: nachos, bread, burgers, or wraps.

Fooddeco
guacamole

GOAT CHEESE GUACAMOLE

1 avocado
¼ cup goat cheese
2 Peppadews, finely chopped
1 tbsp chives, finely chopped
¼ lime, juice and zest
1 tsp chili flakes
1 tsp sushi vinegar
Salt and pepper to taste
Toast
Edible flowers

Halve the avocado and remove the pit and peel. Mash half of the avocado and the goat cheese using a fork. Save the other half to create an avocado rose (page 11). Add the remaining ingredients to the avocado and goat cheese mixture and season with salt and pepper. Scoop the avocado into a small bowl or spread onto toast and place the avocado rose and edible flowers on top.

CURRIED GUACAMOLE

2 avocados
½ lime, juice and zest
1 tbsp yellow curry paste
4 tbsp cilantro, finely chopped
2 tbsp coconut oil, melted
1–2 cloves garlic, finely chopped
½ spring onion, finely chopped
Salt to taste

Halve the avocados and remove the pits and peels. Place the avocados in a bowl and mash them together with all remaining ingredients. Make it as coarse or smooth as you like.

Taste and season with salt.

♥ To make an additional avocado rose (page 11), use half of another avocado.

WASABI GUACAMOLE

2 avocados
1 tsp wasabi paste
1 tbsp pickled ginger, finely chopped
1 tbsp juice from the pickled ginger jar
1 spring onion, finely chopped
2 tbsp fresh cilantro, finely chopped
½ lime, juice and zest
1 clove garlic, finely chopped
1 tsp chili flakes

Cut the avocados in half and remove the pits and peels. Place the avocados in a bowl and using a fork mash them together with all remaining ingredients. Make it as coarse or smooth as you like. Taste and season with chili flakes, wasabi, or salt!

Paired well with rice cakes.

MISO GUACAMOLE

2 avocados
1 tbsp miso
½ lime, juice and zest
½ tsp fresh ginger, finely chopped
1 tsp chili flakes
1 tbsp cilantro, finely chopped
3 kaffir lime leaves, finely chopped
½ clove garlic, finely chopped
1 spring onion, finely chopped
Salt and pepper to taste

Cut the avocados in half and remove the pits and peels. Place the avocados in a bowl and, using a fork, mash them together with all remaining ingredients. Make it as coarse or smooth as you like. Taste and season with salt or pepper!

AVOCADO TEMPURA FRIES WITH GINGER MAYONNAISE

2 avocados
Sunflower oil for frying
Salt to taste

ESSENTIAL FOR THE GINGER MAYONNAISE
3 tbsp mayonnaise
2 tbsp ginger sauce or glaze
1 tsp curry powder
Salt to taste

ESSENTIAL FOR THE TEMPURA BATTER
¾ cup tempura flour
Toppings: lime zest and segments, fresh cilantro

Slice the avocados in half and remove pits and peels. Cut each avocado half into eight "fries," approximately 16 fries per avocado. Place the fries on a cutting board (or dish), on a sheet of baking paper and place in the freezer for 30 minutes.

Meanwhile, mix together the ginger mayonnaise ingredients. Make the tempura batter by mixing the tempura flour and water to a smooth batter. Loosely toss the fries in the tempura batter. Fry for a few minutes in the pan with an inch of sunflower oil until crispy. Work in portions and let the fries dry on a paper towel. Decorate the dish with lime zest, a few lime segments, and cilantro. Perhaps add a pinch of salt. Serve the ginger mayonnaise on the side.

AVOCADO FRIES WITH CHORIZO MAYONNAISE

1 egg
2–3 tbsp flour
⅓ cup Parmesan cheese, finely grated
⅔ cup coarse panko bread crumbs
1 long avocado
Sunflower oil for frying

ESSENTIAL FOR THE MAYONNAISE
½ cup chorizo sausage
3 tbsp mayonnaise

To start on the mayonnaise, cut the chorizo into small cubes and cook until crispy in the frying pan.

To make the avocado fries, in one bowl add one raw scrambled egg, to another bowl add the flour, and in another bowl mix the Parmesan cheese and bread crumbs. Cut the avocado in half and remove the pit and peel. Cut each half into eight long "fries." Dip the avocado fries in the flour, remove any excess flour, and proceed by dipping it in the egg, followed by the bread crumb and Parmesan mixture.

Make sure all avocado fries are covered evenly. In a pan with a thin layer of sunflower oil, fry the avocado fries until they are golden brown on all sides. Remove the cooked chorizo cubes from the pan, keep the oil, and blend the meat to a fine crumble. Add mayonnaise and finish by adding the chorizo oil to the blend. Dry the fries on a piece of paper towel and serve immediately.

5

#SWEETS

AVOCADO-CHOCOLATE CAKE

1 loaf

1 cup dark chocolate, finely chopped
2 cups finely chopped unroasted, unsalted nuts
  (walnuts, pistachios, and almonds)
1 cup dates, finely chopped
3 avocados, peeled and pitted
5 eggs, yolks and whites separated
3 tbsp honey
1 lemon, zest
1 serving espresso
Salt to taste
Coconut oil to grease the baking paper
Optional (as in the photo): 1 banana

♥ **Use an extra banana if you wish to decorate your cake, just as depicted. This gives it a nice touch. Cut the banana lengthwise and place it on top of the cake before you place the cake in the oven.**

Preheat the oven to 350°F. Mix the chocolate and nuts in a food processor to a coarse crumble. Scoop the crumble into a bowl. Grind the dates in a food processor to a purée, then add the avocados, egg yolks, and honey and mix everything until combined. Add the crumble to the batter and stir this together with the lemon zest, espresso, and a pinch of salt until well mixed together.

Beat the egg whites until they form stiff peaks and fold them into the batter. Grease a sheet of baking paper with coconut oil and add the greased baking paper to a 9 x 5-inch baking pan. Spoon in the batter and bake the cake for about 60 minutes in the oven. It is ready when you poke it with a toothpick and it comes out dry. Let the cake cool down first before cutting into it. Store it in the refrigerator.

♥ Instead of sea salt you can also decorate the brownie with basil, edible flowers, or frosting!

♥ Always serve the raw brownie cold straight out of the refrigerator.

RAW BROWNIE
1 brownie

1¼ cup walnuts (unroasted)
1 avocado, peeled and pitted
½ cup honey
½ cup coconut oil, melted
3 tbsp cocoa powder

NEEDED FOR THE TOPPING
½ cup pure chocolate
Sea salt
Optional: edible flowers

Grind the walnuts finely in a food processor until a flour consistency is reached. Add all brownie ingredients except for the topping ingredients and stir to a nice, even mixture. Add extra cocoa powder to taste. Spoon the mixture into an 8 x 4-inch baking paper–lined baking tin. Smooth out the top with the back of a spoon. For the topping, melt the pure chocolate, pour it over the avocado-nut mixture, and sprinkle with sea salt. Leave the raw brownie to harden at a minimum of 2 hours, covered, in the refrigerator. Store the brownie in the refrigerator and cut it with a sharp, warm knife into pieces. Do not leave the brownie out of the refrigerator for too long or it will melt.

CHOCO NICE CREAM

Serves 1–2

You might think that this recipe is packed with cream, chocolate, and sugar, but you couldn't be more wrong. This dessert can be eaten guilt-free for breakfast—if you use the healthy toppings. Using only four ingredients, it can be made very quickly. Note: the bananas must be frozen for at least 4 hours prior to making this recipe.

2 bananas
1 avocado
½ cup almond milk, unsweetened
2–3 tbsp cocoa powder
Toppings (as in the picture): donuts, frosting,
    marshmallows, edible flowers
Extra toppings: pistachios, mint, frozen fruit, granola

Peel the bananas and dice into pieces. Freeze for a minimum of 4 hours, preferably overnight. Cut the avocado in half and remove the pit and peel. In a food processor blend all the ingredients, except for the toppings, to a smooth consistency. Divide the ice cream into two bowls, add a delicious topping, and serve immediately!

75

SUPERFOOD BANANA GARDEN

2 serves

½ avocado
1 banana

TOPPINGS (TO YOUR LIKING)
Pomegranate seeds
Chia seeds
Walnuts
Blackberries
Fresh mint
Goji berries
Cocoa powder

Cut the avocado in half and remove the pit and the skin. Finely mash the avocado using a fork. Cut the banana in half lengthwise.

Smear both halves of the banana with avocado and decorate it with an endless variety of toppings: almonds, pistachios, shredded coconut, sweet cress, cocoa beans, mulberries, granola, and so much more!

♥ You can vary endlessly with the following toppings: almonds, pistachio nuts, shredded coconut, sweet cress, cacao nibs, mulberries, granola, and so on. This is the perfect recipe to let children decorate their own food while giving them a high dose of vitamins.

BROWNIE-DOUGH POWER BALLS

8 balls

½ avocado
3 tbsp almond meal
3 tbsp oat flour, super fine
1 tbsp coconut oil
8 dates, pitted, finely chopped
3 tbsp cocoa powder

DIP TIPS:
Oreos (finely blended), grated coconut, salted pistachios (finely blended), chia seeds

Blend all the ingredients, except for the dips, until everything is finely blended and mixed together. Make eight balls from the mix and dip them in the dip tips mentioned above. Let the balls set in the refrigerator. Eat as many as you like, guilt free!

♥ **Store the power balls, covered, in the refrigerator or keep them stocked in your freezer.**

AVOCADO BOUNTY

1 bounty

My love for cooking and food styling has passed on to my eldest daughter, Mae. She loves this bounty. A part of the fun is decorating it.

1 avocado
¾ cup shredded coconut
½ cup honey
½ cup coconut oil (melted)
½ cup pure chocolate
Optional: edible dried rose petals, sprinkles, chocolate, mini marshmallows

Mix all ingredients except the chocolate and optional toppings in a food processor until combined. Spoon the coconut mixture into a small baking tin (8 x 8 inches) lined with parchment paper. Use the back of a spoon to make the top of the bounty as smooth as possible.

Meanwhile, melt the chocolate. Mix it into the coconut mixture and top with dried rose petals or other toppings of choice. Leave the bounty covered in the refrigerator for at least 2 hours to set.

Keep this avocado bounty in the refrigerator and cut with a sharp (possibly warm) knife to break it into pieces. Do not leave the bounty out of the refrigerator for too long stand because it melts!

♥ Yes, it really is that easy. You can store the bounty (if it lasts that long!) for 5 days in the refrigerator.

♥ Always serve the diced bounty cold, immediately out of the refrigerator.

Conversion Charts

METRIC AND IMPERIAL CONVERSIONS

(These conversions are rounded for convenience)

Ingredient	Cups/Tablespoons/Teaspoons	Ounces	Grams/Milliliters
Butter	1 cup/ 16 tablespoons/ 2 sticks	8 ounces	230 grams
Cheese, shredded	1 cup	4 ounces	110 grams
Cornstarch	1 tablespoon	0.3 ounce	8 grams
Cream cheese	1 tablespoon	0.5 ounce	14.5 grams
Flour, all-purpose	1 cup/1 tablespoon	4.5 ounces/0.3 ounce	125 grams/8 grams
Flour, whole wheat	1 cup	4 ounces	120 grams
Fruit, dried	1 cup	4 ounces	120 grams
Fruits or veggies, chopped	1 cup	5 to 7 ounces	145 to 200 grams
Fruits or veggies, puréed	1 cup	8.5 ounces	245 grams
Honey, maple syrup, or corn syrup	1 tablespoon	0.75 ounce	20 grams
Liquids: cream, milk, water, or juice	1 cup	8 fluid ounces	240 milliliters
Oats	1 cup	5.5 ounces	150 grams
Salt	1 teaspoon	0.2 ounces	6 grams
Spices: cinnamon, cloves, ginger, or nutmeg (ground)	1 teaspoon	0.2 ounce	5 milliliters
Sugar, brown, firmly packed	1 cup	7 ounces	200 grams
Sugar, white	1 cup/1 tablespoon	7 ounces/0.5 ounce	200 grams/12.5 grams
Vanilla extract	1 teaspoon	0.2 ounce	4 grams

OVEN TEMPERATURES

Fahrenheit	Celsius	Gas Mark
225°	110°	¼
250°	120°	½
275°	140°	1
300°	150°	2
325°	160°	3
350°	180°	4
375°	190°	5
400°	200°	6
425°	220°	7
450°	230°	8

Cover design by Mona Lin
Cover photo by Colette Dike